The Caged Owl

Books by Gregory Orr

POETRY

Orpheus & Eurydice (Copper Canyon Press, 2001)
City of Salt (University of Pittsburgh Press, 1995)
New & Selected Poems (Wesleyan Univeristy Press, 1988)
We Must Make a Kingdom of It (Wesleyan University Press, 1986)
The Red House (Harper & Row, 1980)
Gathering the Bones Together (Harper & Row, 1975)
Burning the Empty Nests (Harper & Row, 1973)

CRITICISM

Poetry as Survival (University of Georgia Press, 2002)
Poets Teaching Poets: Self and the World (edited by Voigt and Orr,
    University of Michigan Press, 1996)
Richer Entanglements: Essays and Notes on Poetry and Poems
    (University of Michigan Press, 1993)
Stanley Kunitz: An Introduction to the Poetry (Columbia University
    Press, 1985)

MEMOIR

The Blessing (Council Oak Books, 2002)

The Caged Owl

NEW AND SELECTED POEMS

Gregory Orr

Copper Canyon Press

ACKNOWLEDGMENTS

Versions of some of the new poems appeared in the following magazines:
American Poetry Review, The Boston Book Review, Controlled Burn,
DoubleTake, Luna, Meridian, Poetry, Ploughshares,
Provincetown Arts, Washington Square.

Poems reprinted from *City of Salt* by permission
of the University of Pittsburgh Press.

Poems selected from *We Must Make a Kingdom of It* (1986) and
the new section of a subsequent book, *New & Selected Poems* (1988)
have been blended together as the fifth chapter of this book.

Printed in the United States of America.

Cover art: *Landscape and Void,* 1983, gouache on Chinese paper by Leo Kenney,
Museum of Northwest Art, promised gift of Marshall and Helen Hatch.

Copper Canyon Press is in residence under the auspices of the Centrum
Foundation at Fort Worden State Park in Port Townsend, Washington. Centrum
sponsors artist residencies, education workshops for Washington State students
and teachers, blues, jazz, and fiddle tunes festivals, classical music
performances, and The Port Townsend Writers' Conference.

LIBRARY OF CONGRESS CATALOGING-IN-PUBLICATION DATA

Orr, Gregory.
The caged owl: new and selected poems / by Gregory Orr.
p. cm.
Includes biographical references.
ISBN 1-55659-177-2 (pbk.: alk. paper)
I. Title. PS3565.R7 C34 2002
811'.54 — DC21 2001006504

3 5 7 9 8 6 4 2
FIRST PRINTING

COPPER CANYON PRESS
Post Office Box 271
Port Townsend, Washington 98368
www.coppercanyonpress.org

CONTENTS

New Poems

from

Burning the Empty Nests (*1973*)

from

Gathering the Bones Together (*1975*)

from

We Must Make a Kingdom of It (*1986*)

and

New & Selected Poems (*1988*)

from

City of Salt (*1995*)

from

Orpheus & Eurydice (2001)

The Caged Owl

New Poems

Heart

Its hinges rustless,
restless; opening
and shutting on trust.

—

We guard it;
it guides us.
Gods lack it.
Vacant their gaze.

—

Doctors listen
to its cryptic
lisp.
    From *sacred*
to *scared* — a few
beats skipped,
a letter slipped.

—

Cavity and spasm;
a spark can start
it; parting stop it.

Such a radiant husk
to hive our dust!

Here

Here's green, here's the tree
of being
showing the world
renews itself:
these leaves are proof.

Here's the abyss
waiting with its
kiss of shiver
and bliss.

This is the picnic
under the stars; this
is the portrait of grief:
what we are.

(Trauma) Storm

Hunkered down, nerve-numb,
in the carnal hut,
the cave of self,
while outside a storm
rages.
      Huddled there,
rubbing together
white sticks of
your own ribs,
praying for sparks
in that dark
where tinder is heart,
where tender is not.

Screaming Out Loud

Before, you curled inward
around hurts and scars;
braille of battles
seldom won; fissures
and wristroads
a razor made.
               Stutter
from tongue-stump
unable to utter
its woe.
            Still,
your body was mostly
intact, and you
told yourself:
I'm a lucky husk.

And now, you're shattered,
hurtled outward:
shrapnel of stars
and a weird music:
bone in the wind's throat.

Tin Cup

Here's a tin cup
furred with rust.
Here's a bad heart
I've lugged this far.

Begging? No.
Hauling with me
all a mortal has.

You think I'm grim
and thin, wizened
as a dry stick.
You think I've come
to bore you
with a long story
of torment.

And yet I swear
I love this earth
that scars and scalds,
that burns my feet.

And even hell is holy.

Bolt from the Blue

1. BOLT FROM THE BLUE

Gash in the azure
fabric —

Lightning crack
of ravish.
What's touched
is trashed —
ash and blast.

To rip the sky
then vanish.

Tatterflag
I raise —
shredded blue
above
dazed battlements.

2. STRUCK

To die and yet
live after —

how hide
that shatter?

what mask
of bold
or blank to wear?

3. NEITHER

Zigzag nerve zap —
harsh torch-touch
that scorched
like a skim of frost,
turned bones
to smoke — it
scarred the heart most.

Can't halt what starts
from that marring —

jarred into knowledge
of gist and pith,
crux and thrust,
it keeps
a tight grip;
neither weaker
nor stronger,
but wiser, harder.

4. ELEMENTAL SCAR

First choice —
to nurse
or spurn
the hurt?

Second,
how live
with all
the soft
parts
burned away?

Bare tree
branded
on the heart—
dry twigs
and wizening.

Neither sun
nor rain
assists—
to grow
at all
is to grow
slowly:
to force
the petals,
to *will*
the buds to leaf.

5. THE DANCE

That lightning stroke—
a rainbow bolt—
tore right through you
and is already
speeding past the stars.

All this you see—
dance of dazzle
and debris—is aftermath.

What I'm Saying

What I'm saying isn't exactly news
and to say it bluntly is no big deal:
once you decide to live, you have to lose.

But what if you could simply refuse
by claiming that life itself isn't real?
What I'm saying isn't exactly news —

the Buddhists think this world, hooked on adieus,
is just red dust. If that's true, why feel
that having to live you also have to lose?

Well, because we're bodies, bodies whose
mortal bruise is time's kiss and time's seal.
What I'm saying isn't exactly news.

The luckiest among us live in twos.
Yet love has tied them to a burning wheel
once they decide to live. They have to lose

because time's only tempo is the blues.
It's what we're born to, what our prayers conceal.
What I'm saying isn't exactly news —
once you decide to live, you have to lose.

The River

I felt both pleasure and a shiver
as we undressed on the slippery bank
and then plunged into the wild river.

I waded in; she entered as a diver.
Watching her pale flanks slice the dark
I felt both pleasure and a shiver.

Was this a source of the lake we sought, giver
of itself to that vast, blue expanse?
We'd learn by plunging into the wild river

and letting the current take us wherever
it willed. I had that yielding to thank
for how I felt both pleasure and a shiver.

But what she felt and saw I'll never
know: separate bodies taking the same risk
by plunging together into the wild river.

Later, past the rapids, we paused to consider
if chance or destiny had brought us here;
whether it was more than pleasure and a shiver
we'd found by plunging into the wild river.

Paradise

Life is random as a rolled pair of dice.
What those thrown cubes will show no one can know,
yet everyone thinks he wants paradise.

By which she means cool drinks, the largest slice
of all the pies. Money, too. All the dough.
Yet life's random as a rolled pair of dice:

seldom the same number will come up twice
in a row. Still, "Show me the rainbow!"
everyone thinks. He wants a paradise

where everything is calm, sexy, and precise.
Some setting that's removed the risk and woe
of life's randomness, so the pair of dice

(one a burning coal, the other a lump of ice)
cancel each other's extremes. The glow
of what everyone thinks she wants: paradise,

is what ensues: something lukewarm, something "nice."
A world in which volcanoes never blow
isn't my idea of paradise.
Love life's randomness: the rolled pair of dice.

Some Part of the Lyric

Some part of the lyric wants to exclude
the world with all its chaos and grief
and so conceives shapes (a tear, a globe of dew)

whose cool symmetries create a mood
of security. Which is something all need
and so, the lyric's urge to exclude

what hurts us isn't simply a crude
defense, but an embracing of a few
essential shapes: a tear, a globe of dew.

But to what end? Are there clues
in these forms to deeper mysteries
that no good poem should exclude?

What can a stripped art reveal? Is a nude
more naked than the eye can see?
Can a tear freed of salt be a globe of dew?

And most of all — is it something we can use?
Yes, but only as long as its beauty,
like that of a tear or a globe of dew,
reflects the world it meant to exclude.

Some Notes on Shadows

for Sophia

My shadow and I —
the other world
pressing up against
this one — cheek
by jowl.
      Shape
of my grave
right there at my feet.

      —

The shadow each object
casts is its shape
distorted
by mortality,

or simplified
by that fate:
struck dumb
by the knowledge
it will someday vanish.

      —

Does the shadow
emerge from the object
or the object from the shadow?
Which came first —
the chicken or the tomb?
the womb or the egg?

      —

I walked at the very edge
of a high cliff—
for once,
my shadow
was nowhere
to be seen.

—

Is there anyone among us
who casts no shadow?
Even the clear glass
full of water...
even the water itself.

—

Here is the object.
Here is its shadow.
Which is more real?

—

In the evening,
my shadow is a pool
I dive into:
no splash,
no ripples;
the deep breath
lasts for hours.

—

When I was young
my mother gave me
her favorite books
to read. For every

page of light,
there was another
written in shadows.

—

A shadow completes its object
as death completes life,
as the ocean completes a wave,
as dessert completes a meal.

None of the above.

—

My shadow: gray wing
that longs to lift
my body.
                 With
only one, flight
is impossible.

I walked restlessly
about; my whole
life was a journey
because my shadow
compelled me to search
for its lost companion.

—

In the empty parking lot
the tree's shadow
was an inverted goblet,
was the bottom half
of an hourglass
filled with ash.

—

The shadow of a stone
can tell the hour,
but it cannot tell the day.

—

Sometimes it seems
to have disappeared
entirely, to have shrunk
to nothing under
the noonday sun.

Yet I know it's become
a shaft beneath my feet
as if I stood
poised in the air
balanced on a column
of pure absence —
my body become a statue
erected by those
who love me most
and mourn my loss.

—

According to Zeno,
a father's shadow
is twice as long
as his son's,
and the son's twice
as long as his son's,
and therefore
time is impossible,
movement an illusion,

and it would be best
never to have been born.

—

All shapes and sizes
they walk by:
three plump Mennonite girls
in their checked dresses
and white caps,
the blond shopgirl
in black leggings,
a portly worker
with lumbering gait,
holding his coffee
in one hand like a lantern.

Each with his shadow,
each with her shadow.

—

Whatever she said,
her shadow unsaid.
What she offered,
her shadow withheld.

The door she opened,
her shadow closed.
The kiss she gave,
her shadow took back.

—

I love my shadow
more than my shadow
loves me.

Thus
hopeless longing—
thus intimacy
forever proposed,
forever postponed
(and the long journey begun).

—

His stone knows the day
of his birth, knows also
the day of his death.
Its shadow knows nothing
yet covers all the rest.

—

I stood on the threshold
of the grave.
My shadow fell on one side
then the other,
swaying back and forth
like high grass in wind,
like waterweeds
in a stream.
          As if
having guided me this far
it was suddenly uncertain.

—

If shadows could talk
they would tell us
everything we know already
but in the melodious
language of tears
in which every third word rhymes.

—

I had two brothers
who died as little kids.
Sometimes the one
is my shadow,
sometimes the other.

—

My shadow and I
raced across
a landscape of dreams.

Who would tire first?
Who would give up?
Who would give in?

—

(what the shadow said)

I am the voice
beneath your voice.
I am the echo
of your mortal shell.
When you drink a toast
to life, I lift
a glass to the dead.

—

The shadow a skull casts
on bare ground
is as nothing
to the congregation
of shadows it hoards.

—

Certain shadows are transparent,
invisible—like a flying
buttress made of glass
propping up
a collapsing cathedral;
dangerous to walk too close
to such a structure.

—

The History of Shadows
was written by light.
The History of Light
was written by shadows.

The only two books
in the Library of Time,
yet no one comes
to borrow or browse
these dusty tomes.

—

I sat at my desk,
pen in hand.
What my shadow spoke,
I wrote.

Was I wrong?
Should I
have argued more?

—

When the shadow cast
by my past
meets the shadow
cast by my future,
I become the door
that opens
both ways, I become
the conch shell
at the water's edge:
one ocean outside me,
the other within.

—

If objects are notes
of a melody,
their shadows
are the instruments
that play the song.
Low notes
of the pine tree
emerging from its blue cello.
The saltshaker
on the kitchen table—
its tiny violin.

The Journey

for Jane Kenyon (1947–1995)

Beside me on the plane
an old woman reads
a green pocket Bible,
its tissue pages
thin as a fly's wing.
Below, the Monagahela
winds among smokestacks
and morning fog.

I've left behind my students,
a final exam
someone else must present:

*Why do you write? What
does poetry mean?
Does it have a purpose
beyond the personal?*

    —

Out past my own grief
I hear your lyrics
shaping pain
or giving joy the name
of some common flower:
daffodil, peony, Queen Anne's lace.

What the self extends: leaf
by leaf, or the whole
blossom at once,
pattern we can't explain.

    —

Long ago, a teacher told me
of a poetry contest in Spain.
Third prize: a silver rose;
second, a gold.
               The winner
held her real rose,
the earth already
calling its petals home.

Fall

A day so lovely it could be Eden
on the first day, when the beasts got their names
and Adam stood there naked with his pen.

God led each animal forward and then
Adam stared deep in its eyes. Such games
they played on a lovely day in Eden.

They didn't care, the beasts of hill and den;
they knew who they were. Imperial claims
poor Adam made, naked but for his pen,

were like a brand-new joke to them. What men
would call them as they killed them was a shame
not theirs to bear on that day in Eden.

Yet how solemn God and Adam looked when
they spoke the words. And so, the beasts went tame,
trying to please poor Adam and his pen.

Now fur and claw move far beyond our ken.
Shed blood's between. It hasn't been the same
since that long-lost, lovely day in Eden
when Adam stood there naked with his pen.

Two Poems about Nothing

Now I will write a song about nothing at all....
GUILLAUME IX OF AQUITAINE (1071–1127)

When I was young
I fell in love
with nothing.
Nothing had
my heart.
I was a moody
unpleasant youth;
even my mother
disliked me.
What are you
brooding about?
she'd ask.
      Nothing,
I'd answer.
For once, she
approved.
You're good
for nothing,
she said, and
nothing is good
enough for you.

—

When I was a child
nothing was everywhere.
It lay thick on leaves
and gathered in pools
under cedar trees.
Nothing filled
our barns
and grazed our pastures.

Nothing was so abundant
we never thought
to praise or prize it.
Those days are gone
forever. Now nothing
is scarce
and we lack for nothing.

Nothing and the Incident in the Streets

South Carolina State University, Orangeburg, 1968

National Autonomous University of Mexico,
Mexico City, 1968

Tiananmen Square, Beijing, China, 1989

Nothing forced those kids
to go out there.
Nothing made them insist
on their foolish demands.

—

Those kids believed in nothing.
They respected nothing,
you could see that by the way
they behaved.

Nothing mattered to them
once they got excited.

When we were young, nothing
like this
could have happened.
We knew nothing was worth
this much trouble.

—

Nothing told them to go home
before it was too late.
Nothing scolded them
for the foolish children
they were. Nothing warned them
of the serious consequences.
Nothing said: This is not

a carnival or celebration,
but a serious threat to the state.

—

Nothing proceeded
exactly according
to the rules.

The police arrived.
They followed orders
precisely.

Nothing was left
to chance.
Nothing had been
anticipated
by our rulers
down to the last
numbered hair
on the protesters'
heads,
down to the last
sparrow's feather.

Nothing took place
that shouldn't have.

Nothing went wrong.

—

Nothing could have prepared
us for what happened next.
It could have, but
it didn't. Nothing
like it had been seen before.

But not by us.
We were surprised and shocked
by all the blood. Nothing
could have surprised us more.

—

Nothing was seen of them again.
Nothing was heard of them.
Nothing was mentioned
in the press.
          By dawn
of the next day
the authorities had already
scrubbed the streets,
painted over the graffiti,
and removed the posters.

Nothing came of their demands.

Their sacrifice changed
nothing. Nothing
was the same afterwards.
Nothing went on as usual.
Nothing was different
than it had ever been.

—

It's easy enough, after
it's over, to demand:
Why didn't you do
something?

If you had been there
you would have seen
nothing could have

prevented it. Nothing
could have stepped in
and stopped it.

Nothing had the power
to halt it right there.
So we waited for nothing.
And nothing arrived
in the nick of time.
Nothing kept the bullets
back. Nothing stood
like a wall between
the rifles
and their human targets.
Nothing saved them.

—

Darkness of human
hearts. Only
following orders.
Caught up
in the moment's
excitement.
A small, necessary
wrong for a higher
cause.
          Are these
excuses or explanations?

They tell us nothing.

Nothing is the key
to this brutal mystery.
Nothing can explain
what happened there.

Nothing has the power
to get inside their
motives, what drove
them to do such things.
Nothing will tell us
how they justified
to themselves
the shed blood.

Nothing has seen
such shuffling
of masks before:
the mask of regret
replacing the mask
of rage.
                    Nothing
has seen such behavior
since time began.

Nothing will tell us
how they sleep
soundly at night
while others do not
sleep at all, and
others sleep forever.

—

Nothing was further
from the truth.
Not a lot further.
Maybe the distance
of those bodies
laid end to end.

—

The incident was nothing
to speak of.

Nothing we said
would have changed it,

so we said nothing.

—

Nothing cries out
from the clean
streets as if
they were still
bright with blood.
Nothing echoes
like a confusion
of shouts
bouncing off
the silent walls
of buildings.

Nothing will
vindicate them.
Nothing will make
sure they are not
forgotten. Nothing
will be their voice.

A Dream of Fifty

Among all the losses, this was immense:
I dreamed my birthday; I'd just turned fifty.
Wind pressed leaves against the grid of fence,

having scoured them off a lawn dense
with their fleshy falling. And every tree
stood among its losses. This immense

feeling of air in motion. A sense
my suffering was past and I was free.
Wind-pressed leaves against a grid of fence

celebrated my release. Now, laments
were beside the point. As if destiny
said: Of all these losses none is immense

as what you'll gain. Let the new life commence;
let it begin here with this mystery:
wind pressing leaves against the grid of fence;

the kind of image the dreaming mind invents
to help us shed our griefs more easily.
All my losses offset by this: immense
wind pressing leaves against a grid of fence.

Shaky Spectrum

Here's "anguish" and over
there is "dance."
Split the difference
and you have the heart
trapped in the middle,
turning on a spit,
twisting on its spindle...

What to relinquish?
What to give up?
                    The ghost
or its host? The soul
or its embodiment?

Here's a hint: Guess
wrong and you're gone.

You say the heart's torn.

Into how many pieces?

We can't count them now.
Wait till the beast's asleep.

The Talk

for my father

How many years we've circled round this date,
not that it might come, but as a dreaded day.
And now we'll talk, although our talk's too late.

We played our cards, holding back each ace
until your last hand showed the queen of spades.
How many years we've circled round this date.

So "cancer" is the word we cannot say,
and can't not say — it works both ways;
but now we'll talk, although our talk's too late.

What stood between us was never outright hate
but fear so deep it urged us to delay,
and so for years we've circled round this date.

You hobble toward your chair, your lessened weight
propped on a cane. I hold my ground in a daze.
We'll talk, and, talking, pray it's not too late

to change the way we've read our lives as fate.
We hid our love. Now we must hide dismay,
forget the years we've circled round this date,
and talk at last, though all our talk's too late.

The Excavation

for my father, on his
first dig at seventy

1

In this dry, stubble field
a thousand years ago,
a nameless tribe lived
where two rivers joined.

Now with sun pressed
to aching back
you dig through chalk
and marl.

Then down
among the layers you crouch
with a tiny brush.
The shards you seek
no bigger than a thumb,
or bits of bone
to tell you what they ate.

2

To tell you what they ate
I'd have to take you back
to where they sat
at the table: your sons
and daughter.
It might be
early morning, before
the school bus comes,
or evening with dark
pressing down on the fields.

Their mother's been dead
a year now—her presence
less than a whisper.
Your absence is the mystery
their lives close around
as a mouth might close
with a small stone
on the tongue, and so
it's already begun:
their journey to the other world.

3

Their journey to the other world
we might infer from the way
a skeleton's arranged
in a grave, but this
is where they lived
and signs of life
are what we'll find.

I think that dark spot
marks a hearth. I think
your children grew, then
grew apart and made
their isolate ways
into the world.

    I think
you are an old man
searching for artifacts
and what they might reveal,
here where the hole you dug
gives shelter from an unrelenting sun
in this dry, stubble field.

If There's a God...

If there's a god of amphetamine, he's also the god of wrecked lives, and it's only he who can explain how my doctor father, with the gift of healing strangers and patients alike, left so many intimate dead in his wake.

If there's a god of amphetamine, he's also the god of recklessness, and I ask him to answer.

He's the god of thrills, the god of boys riding bikes down steep hills with their hands over their heads.

He's the god of holy and unholy chance, the god of soldiers crossing a field and to the right of you a man falls dead and to the left also and you are still standing.

If there's a god of amphetamine, he's the god of diet pills, who is the god of the fifties housewife who vacuums all day and whose bathroom is spotless and now it is evening as she sits alone in the kitchen, polishing her chains.

He's the god of the rampant mind and the god of my father's long monologues by moonlight in the dark car driving over the dusty roads.

He's the god of tiny, manic orderings in the midst of chaos, the god of elaborate charts where Greg will do this chore on Monday and a different one on Tuesday and all the brothers are there on the chart and all the chores and all the days of the week in a minuscule script no one can read.

If there's a god of amphetamine, my father was his hopped-up acolyte who leapt out of bed one afternoon to chase a mouse through the house, shouting, firing his .38 repeatedly at the tiny beast scurrying along the wall while Jon wailed for help from the next room.

If there's a god of amphetamine, he's the god of subtle carnage and dubious gifts who lives in each small pill that tastes of electricity and dust.

If there's a god of amphetamine, my father was its high priest, praising it, preaching its gospel, lifting it like a host and intoning: "Here in my hand is the mystery: a god alive inside a tiny tablet. He is a high god, a god of highs—he eats the heart to juice the brain and mocks the havoc he makes, laughing at all who stumble. Put out your tongue and receive it."

To My Father, Dying

Where is your scorn now?
Where your jaggedness,
old antagonist?
                    Time
has worn you smooth
as a boulder
tumbled in a stream.
Your handsome face
gone slack;
your thatch of black
hair still thick
but white now, and your
bristly eyebrows, too —
albino spiders poised
above holes in soft sand.

How shall I get on
without you, whose love
like hatred made me a man?

Celestial Desolations

for Marjorie Sargent

Now God wants even
us mollusks
to frolic—
he's sent his bolt
to smash open
that shell that was
my soul's abode.
Now there's no
more hiding, now
the core
of me's exposed.

Blast and shatter;
glitter and gone…

And so the heart
must gather
all its atoms,
glue them
with dew.

And so the world
begins anew:
miracle of molecules
clinging,
the spider
in the dark night
reweaving
its torn web
thread by thread.

Best

The Greeks said: Never to be born is best;
next best, to die young in a noble cause.
"Où sont les neiges d'antan?" Villon asked.

"Where are yesteryear's snows" is, I guess,
the phrase in English. Villon spoke in praise
of women not born when the Greeks said: "Best

not to exist at all." Yet the French poet pressed
on with his list: great beauties of the past.
"Où sont les neiges d'antan?" Villon asked.

In his great poem, only their names persist:
Joan, Beatrice, Blanche of the White Arms.
Were the Greeks right — Not to live at all is best?

What would Blanche's lovers say to this
who are themselves just dust, all suffering
long gone as the snows after which Villon asked?

Beauty is like life itself: a dawn mist
the sun burns off. It gives no peace, no rest.
"Où sont les neiges d'antan?" we ask.
But the Greeks were wrong: To live and love is best.

Wild Heart

for Trisha

Where would I be if not for your wild heart?
I ask this not from love, but selfishly —
how could I live? How could I make my art?

Questions I wouldn't ask if I were smart.
Take the whole thing on faith. Blind eyes can see
where I would be if not for your wild heart.

Love or need — who can tell the two apart?
Nor does it matter much, since both agree
that I need you to live and make my art.

Are you the target; am I the bow and dart?
Are you the deer that doesn't want to flee
and turns to give the hunter her wild heart?

I bite the apple and the apple's tart
but that's the complex taste of destiny.
How could I live? How could I make my art

in some bland place like Eden, set apart
from the world's tumult and its agony?
Where would I be if not for your wild heart?
How could I live? How could I make my art?

Paradise Lightning Dazzle

1. PARADISE

Persian word meaning "walled garden"

Pleasure space crammed
with flowers, fountains,
and cool shade —
all the joys
earth affords
hidden behind high walls.

Crack, lightning zap
I press my eye against —
glimpse of paradise
that makes me long for more.

2. TOO BRIGHT

One step beyond
intensity —
what world is that?

Light shining
at the farthest rim
of the visible —

Does it rise
or fall there?

Is that where
it lives, or dies?

3. FULLNESS

Fullness — the overmuch —
ripe teetering
on the brink
of rot.
  Light
so bright
eyes squeezed tight
can't shut it out.

Again and again
the edge is struck —
cymbal that shivers
with the overflow of sight.

4. BOTH

I've been the pear's
green skin
harder
than armor;
and also
the snowflake
even moonlight
can bruise.

And this, too —
our senses crave
intensity,
crave even more
than they can bear.

5. ALMOST A LONELINESS

One and by one
we come to this place.

And those with companions
are also alone.

Sky and earth
and all the world
before us.

It's possible
to imagine the tree,
standing by itself.

But also the flowers—
how the weight
of so much being
bows them down.

6. YES

Burden and blessing—
two blossoms
on the same branch.

To be so lost
in this radiant wilderness.

7. TO SAY

To say "now" and yet again
"now"
as the rose
of each moment
opens toward us,
ransacking
our senses
with its redolent folds.

8. EQUIVALENTS

Here's "bride" and "bridge,"
here's reaching.

Here's "bliss"
casting itself down
to kiss "abyss" —
luminous mist-cloud
the crashing cataract spews.

9. THIS DAZZLING

Was it only
for a single moment
I was lifted up?
Slipped free
of this shroud
that veils my eyes
and weights my limbs?

And saw below me
the pattern,
clear at last:
radiant labyrinth?

10. THAT MIGHT BE

Chaos — this world's
word
for love.

How light
lifts each object
in its gilded,
infinite arms —

insisting it
be brought to birth,
to bursting…

Be-all

The insect clings
to the green
stalk, sucks
its sap,
holds to the world
because it knows
the world is whole
and holy — the be-all
and the end-all
of it.

      But me —
I feel I'm ghost
and gristle
both.
      My sickness
is to think
there's something
out there called
the Infinite —

a place where
all my longing
will become *belong.*

Burning the Empty Nests

1973

Washing My Face

Last night's dreams disappear.
They are like the sink draining:
a transparent rose swallowed by its stem.

Silence

The way the word sinks
into the deep snow of the page.

The deer lying dead
in the clearing,
its head and antlers
transparent.
           The black
seed in its brain
parachuting toward earth.

"Transients Welcome"

To be like the water:
a glass snake asleep in the pipes.
But behind you the dream burns the empty nests,
and before you the day with its ball of twine.
You piss in the sink. Frying pan in hand,
padding down the hall, you turn the corner
and find an old woman asleep on the stove.

The Girl with Eighteen Nightgowns

And each one to the advantage of her breasts
which were present in softness
and under softness
were present
like miniature rabbits in the Andes
that only come out at night.

The Doll

I carry you in a glass jar.
Your face is porcelain
except for the bullet hole
like a black mole on your cheek.
I want to make you whole again,
but you are growing smaller.
It is almost too late.
When I touch you my fingers
leave dark smudges on your skin.
Each day you are growing
smaller and more intense,
like a drop of acid on my palm;
mothball, snowflake,
dead child.

Getting Dressed

1

In the morning, I pull on
my helmet of skin
backwards. I see
what a lightbulb sees
through a lampshade.

2

Putting on the white gloves,
the ones with little teeth
that close around my wrists.

3

Pale feet, two corpses
that will not stay buried,
I thrust you into my boots:
wearing this barbaric armor
you go out to battle the air,
the stones, the earth
that wants to swallow you.

Manhattan Island Poem

Thin river woman with a concrete star
wedged in her ear. I wrap
a blue scarf of old movies around my eyes.
At night I am a jar of fireflies dying.

A Parable

The stone strikes the body, because
that is what stones will do.
The wound opens after the stone's kiss,
too late to swallow the stone.
The wound and the stone become lovers.
The wound owes its life to the stone
and sings the stone's praises.
The stone is moved. At the stone's center,
a red hollow aches to touch the wound.
The gray walls of its body tear open
and the wound enters to dwell there.

A stranger picks up the stone
with the wound inside and carries it
with him until he dies.

The Dinner

I invited Mozart to dinner
on condition he didn't
embarrass me.
In the middle of the meal
he began weeping uncontrollably.
"You silly fuck," I screamed,
"what are you doing
in this century
if you can't take it?"

The Bridge

In the dawn light these white girders
are the bones we want to be free of.

The water calls to me,
saying: Your body is here with us.
Where have you been? We were waiting.
Return to yourself.

Love Poem

A black biplane crashes through the window
of the luncheonette. The pilot climbs down,
removing his leather hood.
He hands me my grandmother's jade ring.
No, it is two robin's eggs and
a telephone number: yours.

The Room

With crayons and pieces of paper,
I entered the empty room.
I sat on the floor and drew pictures all day.
One day I held a picture against the bare wall:
it was a window. Climbing through,

I stood in a sloping field
at dusk. As I began walking, night settled.
Far ahead in the valley, I saw the lights
of a village, and always at my back I felt
the white room swallowing what was passed.

Making Beasts

When I was about ten
I glued together an old
white turtle shell,
a woodchuck's skull,
and a red squirrel's tail
to make my first
mythical beast.
What has been created
is never lost. It crawls
up through my thoughts now
on the feet I never gave it.

Poem to the Mother

Dead leaves nest in the crown and the word
"yesterday" is like a pile of bones.

But is a volcano ever extinct,
even when its bowl fills with snow
and the giant ice deer come there to die?

Kissing you makes the leaves fall.

How they heaped snow in the cradle
of your hips and it didn't melt.
How at your touch the flowers
exploded in flames.

Again we dismantle the motorcycle.
In your arms you rock the black egg of the gas tank.
A beak like golden pliers tears at the thin metal.
Another you is released into the universe.

The Fast

My bones start singing through my skin.
They sing about the other life
when they had teeth of their own.
It is a lie they heard from their father.
They sing all the old lies
as though they were threats.
They think they can frighten me,
because I grow thin.
But I know my rights.
I know the law, the one that says:
The bones of the son belong to the father.
They are his food.

Going Out

You hold your hands up to the light.
The small mirrors of your fingernails
are painted over with blood.
You help me knot the black
tie tight around my throat.
Tonight we are going to dine.
We have a hunger that nothing has filled.
It grows large and rigid.
We stand in it like a room.

Lines Written in Dejection, Oklahoma

I have never lived on the reservation.
Let me put it this way: in the web of my hands
I hold an egg of air.
When the girl gets off the train
I will be alone. Only myself and
the moon with its rivers and thorns.

For me there is no getting off.
The river writes my name on its side.
The train with my name on it races
over the dark fields. And the Indian
silhouetted against the ridge
lifts his pony, flings it at the moon.

Daffodil Poem

I remember the cloud on its blue bicycle
gliding over the leaves under the bare branches.
You and I were walking.
You wore your long green dress
with the hem frayed so the loose threads
seemed like tiny roots.
We were holding hands when my hand
became a yellow scarf
and you stood waving it slowly.
I stepped off the train in Pennsylvania,
just as it began to snow.

Sleeping Alone in a Small Room

There are dawns when the window
is white with moths,
or black with the ink
they spin out of their bodies.

I dream of stones covered with snow.
Or I stand on a hill at night,
counting the fires in the valley.
Once I held a blue cup
shaped like an hourglass.
Looking into it, past the narrow
waist, I saw her small,
child's face staring up from the bottom.

Then there are mornings I wake
between darkness and light
and see the cloud that hangs
by a rope from the steeple
turn red and begin to dance.

October

At my feet the stream flows backwards,
a road through the hills.
But to travel it I would have to be naked,
more naked than I have ever been.

Behind me the red and orange leaves whisper.
I am afraid of the woods in daylight,
the colors demanding I feel.

My hands are cold. I am trapped
between the woods and the water.
"I must face this fear," I think,
and struggle to stay in my body,
but the scream comes, the scream
that is like my hands
only larger, like two wings of ice.

Trying to Sleep

I am too thin. My bones press
against my flesh:
they are trying to break free
and live separate lives
like candles. I try
to think of something else.
I sit up and look out
the window. There is only
the neighbor's black dog
barking at the snow.

Singing the Pain Back into the Wound

I crouch naked at the wound's edge
and call its name softly,
until it hovers over me and I am clothed
in its shadow. Then I throw ropes
over it, pulling it down into the wound
that its body fits perfectly
like a fish-shaped cork.
Its wings beat frantically. I lash them together,
fold them carefully into a black
bundle on its back.

Poem

This life like no other.
The bread rising in the ditches.
The bellies of women swelling
with air.
Walking alone under the dark pines,
a blue leather bridle in my hand.

Beginning

You stand alone in the empty street
and the dark air swept from houses
swirls thickly around your knees.

You remember cutting the white
threads, how a red drop formed
like a tear at each end.
But when you cut the black threads,
the thicker ones, there was a sweet
heavy smell of flowers and urine.

Now you begin. Because your boots
leave no marks on the hard earth,
you will make each journey many times.

from

Gathering the Bones Together

1975

Gathering the Bones Together

for Peter Orr

When all the rooms of the house
fill with smoke, it's not enough
to say an angel is sleeping on the chimney.

1. A NIGHT IN THE BARN

The deer carcass hangs from a rafter.
Wrapped in blankets, a boy keeps watch
from a pile of loose hay. Then he sleeps

and dreams about a death that is coming:
Inside him, there are small bones
scattered in a field among burdocks and dead grass.
He will spend his life walking there,
gathering the bones together.

Pigeons rustle in the eaves.
At his feet, the German shepherd
snaps its jaws in its sleep.

2

A father and his four sons
run down a slope toward
a deer they just killed.
The father and two sons carry
rifles. They laugh, jostle,
and chatter together.
A gun goes off
and the youngest brother
falls to the ground.
A boy with a rifle
stands beside him,
screaming.

3

I crouch in the corner of my room,
staring into the glass well
of my hands; far down
I see him drowning in air.

Outside, leaves shaped like mouths
make a black pool
under a tree. Snails glide
there, little death-swans.

4. SMOKE

Something has covered the chimney
and the whole house fills with smoke.
I go outside and look up at the roof,
but I can't see anything.
I go back inside. Everyone weeps,
walking from room to room.
Their eyes ache. This smoke
turns people into shadows.
Even after it is gone
and the tears are gone,
we will smell it in pillows
when we lie down to sleep.

5

He lives in a house of black glass.
Sometimes I visit him, and we talk.
My father says he is dead,
but what does that mean?
Last night I found a child
sleeping on a nest of bones.
He had a red, leaf-shaped
scar on his cheek.

I lifted him up
and carried him with me,
though I didn't know where I was going.

6. THE JOURNEY

Each night, I knelt on a marble slab
and scrubbed at the blood.
I scrubbed for years and still it was there.
But tonight the bones in my feet
begin to burn. I stand up
and start walking, and the slab
appears under my feet with each step,
a white road only as long as your body.

7. THE DISTANCE

The winter I was eight, a horse
slipped on the ice, breaking its leg.
Father took a rifle, a can of gasoline.
I stood by the road at dusk and watched
the carcass burning in the far pasture.

I was twelve when I killed him;
I felt my own bones wrench from my body.
Now I am twenty-seven and walk
beside this river, looking for them.
They have become a bridge
that arches toward the other shore.

A Life

At dawn you curl up in the top branches
and sleep.
All day you are a cloud.
Birds fly through it.

At dusk animals gather at the waterhole
as if to drink,
but it has become a mirror,
because you are dreaming:
                    At your feet
glass has replaced water, the way
words have replaced feeling.

All night you sit in the tree, listening
to the howl and moan of the animals
in the darkness below.

The Cage

After its capture, the animal
was caged in a room of mirrors.
Staring at itself, it began
to shed great clumps of fur.
To save itself, it learned
to close its left eye,
hiding that half of its body.
Its right side shriveled up,
but its left hand
seized things and continued to grow.

The Snail

The snail sat in the blind man's palm.
The man remembered Helen Keller's dream:
that she held a pearl in her hand,
and she "saw" it,
the most beautiful thing in her life.
"What is a snail?" the blind man asked.
It is a pearl that dies.
You can find its empty shell
at the foot of a tree in the woods
like a white ear that is listening.

Two Lines from the Brothers Grimm

for Larry and Judy Raab

Now we must get up quickly,
dress ourselves, and run away.
Because it surrounds us, because
they are coming with wolves on leashes,
because I stood just now at the window
and saw the wall of hills on fire.
They have taken our parents away.
Downstairs in the half dark, two strangers
move about, lighting the stove.

The Hats

The hats are hungry.
What will they eat?
The funny uncle
puts his hand into his hat
and pulls out an empty sleeve.
All the parents are laughing,
but the children are scared.
What will the hats eat now;
the hats our fathers wear?
See the hat in the corner.
Has it been fed?

Domestic Life

1. TODAY

Open yourself up: today
that's no different than opening
a refrigerator door: large chunks
of meat, eggs
scattered on the metal racks,
and cowering in the back:
a tiny, frightened woman.
You are huge and clumsy;
you fumble for her, breaking
all the eggs, and she eludes you,
and you don't feel a thing
except cold inside.

2. SOMETHING

Something is burning inside you
like a rose made from cellophane,
like something white burning
in a snowfield: no flames,
all you can see is the shadow
of smoke on the snow.

3. BEFORE DAWN

Your wife left before you woke.
She scratched a note on your back;
you try to read it with mirrors.

You decide to talk to the cat,
but when you open your mouth
honey-colored wasps fly out.

The blood in the lightbulbs
burns less brightly.

4. THE WATERFALL

Failing to hold on to things,
a man can become
a waterfall.
His friends stare,
silent and aghast,
as he disappears
over the cliff, carrying
off his books, his wife,
all his furniture.

5. FALL CLEANING

This morning, the almost weightless bodies
of insects drift down
from the ceiling. It's seasonal;
you have to expect that sort of thing
when you live in a burrow under the earth.
Yesterday a package arrived
in the mail; it contained bird beaks
in assorted colors and sizes.
Some are small like yellow thorns,
but others are larger;
I slip those over my fingers,
clack them together and dance
around the room in my gray bathrobe.
The insects revive. I am their god.
They dance after me up the tunnel
and out into the autumn woods.

The King of the Earthworms

Waking each day, always
at the end of a tunnel,
dirt pressed against my face.
I move by taking a bite,
chewing my way
through the packed rubble
of earth, roots, and bones.
Like Chuang Tzu's butterfly,
I cherish an alternate life:
that of a man
who lies down to sleep;
one wall of his room disappears
and the mattress floats out
into the night air.

The Sweater

I will lose you. It is written
into this poem the way
the fisherman's wife knits
his death into the sweater.

A Large White Rock Called "The Sleeping Angel"

He lay down in this field to rest.
Seeing an ant carry
a white egg the size of a rice grain,
the angel believed it was a sign
the animals of this world
wanted to make him their king.
While he slept, sheep licked
his salt wings.
Only these stubs remain.

All Morning

All morning the dream lingers.
I am like thick grass
in a meadow, still
soaked with dew at noon.

The Builders

for Trisha

Midnight: the field becomes white stone.
We quarry it. We carry the cut squares
strapped to our backs.

On the side of a bleak hill
we build our hut: windowless,
but filled with light.

Overtaken by Fog While Climbing

Mount Chikora, New Hampshire

The path at my feet disappears
in thick mist.
I sit down on a rock and wait.
To pass the time, I stare
at my hand floating
far away at the end of its sleeve
like a white plant root;
it doesn't seem attached
even to its own wrist.
It is hard to love this thing,
so frail and alien.

Like Any Other Man

I was born with a knife
in one hand
and a wound in the other.

In the house where I lived
all the mirrors
were painted black.

So many years
before the soft key of your tongue
unlocked my body.

The Red House

1980

The Lost Children

Years ago, as dusk seeped from the blue
spruce in the yard, they ran to hide.
It was easy to find those who crouched
in the shadow of the chicken coop
or stood still among motionless
horses by the water trough.
But I never found the willful
ones who crossed the fence and lay
down in the high grass to stare up
at the pattern of stars
and meandering summer firefly sparks.

Now I stand again by the fence
and pluck one rusted strand of wire,
harp of lost worlds. At the sound
the children rise from hiding
and move toward me:
eidolons, adrift on the night air.

from

THE RED HOUSE

Fair seed-time had my soul, and I grew up
Fostered alike by beauty and by fear....
WORDSWORTH, *The Prelude*, BOOK I

Morning Song

Sun on his face wakes him.
The boy makes his way down
through the spidery dark
of stairs to his breakfast
of cereal in a blue bowl.
He carries to the barn
a pie plate heaped
with vegetable scraps
for the three-legged deer.
As a fawn it stood still
and alone in high hay
while the red tractor
spiraled steadily inward,
mowing its precise swaths.
"I lived" is the song
the boy hears as the deer
hobbles toward him.
In the barn's huge gloom
light falls through cracks
the way sword blades
pierce a magician's box.

The Ditch

for Don Hall and Jane Kenyon

1

All his eighth spring he watched
a toy-size yellow backhoe and dozer
chuff and groan in the shallow valley
behind his house. They gouged a line
through swampy bottomland he loved,
draining it to make pasture for cows.

2

By early summer the ditch was full.
He tromped along it, sweltering
in hipboots, hunting turtles.
When he saw one he plunged
and plucked it from the orange water:
spotted turtles, painted turtles,
and sometimes a snapper whose jaws
he'd tease shut on a stick,
then drag out by its notched tail.
From lacquery shells he scraped
leeches, then placed each turtle
on top of a hillock the backhoe
left. Beak hooked like a hawk's,
lidded eyes: the head pulled in
with a hiss now slowly emerged.

3

August; the swamp was gone.
He strolled between high reeds
along muskrat channels: dry
paths in a formal garden.
And the small pond's bottom

was baked, cracked, curled up
into little plates of clay.
When he paused beside them
bluebottle flies didn't budge,
magnetized to the gleaming
scales of a carp.

4

The three-chambered hearts of the turtles
pushed slow blood. Secure under layers
of late-autumn mud they drowsed.

He climbed over fallen willow limbs
and traversed a stubble field at dusk,
carrying with him their dream of spring.

He heard the dinner bell his mother rang;
he saw his father's red car crossing
the flats, dragging huge plumes of dust.

Neighbors

1. EDITH

A photo on the mantel:
her Texas Ranger husband,
six years deceased.
She still had his pistol.
In a screened porch
off the bedroom: a hundred
cacti, most so large
they couldn't fit
through the door; all
of them brown, unwatered,
puckered, dead.

2. CHRISTOPHER AUGUSTINOVICH

We were picking strawberries
in the patch behind his shack.
He and I knelt with heads
almost touching as we worked
two sides of a green row.
He jabbered about his youth
in the Czar's army, paused,
looked up and gaped to show:
five yellow stumps
in a reeking cave.
Do you know what did it,
old Chris asked
with a grin and a wink?
Liquor and kissing.

Work Gloves

for Bill and Jon Orr

All morning with gloved
hands, we grip and tug
burdock and the tough
fibrous stalks of chicory.
We knock roots against
bootsoles to jar
the clumped earth loose.

When the brushpile's
tangled mound is high enough
we set it ablaze and stand
squinting into the heat,
waiting for the branch
that always rises whole
and flaming, ready
to sprint to where it settles
and put out its sparks
with quick, flat
slaps of our bamboo rakes.

At dusk, easing down
on porch steps to unlace
my boots, I pause:
smoke, sweat, dirt, and flesh
make this smell I love:
I hold my face in my hands
and breathe deeply.

The Brave Child

How, on a dare, he would dive where the stream
eddied back on itself, down
to a deepest bottom dark with the rot
of logs and leaves, then like a little
Lazarus rise
with the oozing proof clutched in his fist.

Or, on a ladder nailed to the loft wall,
would climb toward a roof where pigeons
rattled and cooed, hang from a beam
high over hay, then,
with arms spread like a Christ ascending,
fall through the dust-filled air.

Adolescence

The dog barks from a cloud
after each car passes
and a fine powder settles
on yard shrubs. In late spring
the county truck sprays
oil on the road, binding
the dust. I strip
catkins from willows
and beat the air
with insane intensity.
Reeds bending in wind;
electrical hum
from a roadside pole.
Behind the red house, gray
clouds and the rumble
of summer thunder. Above,
yellow, spiked globes swell
among the deep green
chestnut leaves. And in the hay,
can't breathe; can't
breathe in the hay. Hands
on skin; how good it feels.

Horses

I brace my knee against
one side of the lifted bale
and tug at twine until
it bursts and loosed hay
tumbles from the high loft
over the bowed heads of horses
waiting in the barn's shadow.

In dream, the red one stands
over my bed, wide-eyed and quiet,
though with her mane afire.
Or galloped across quick fields,
it is her neck that sweats
beneath my hand, her sides
heaving between my thighs.

Sunday School Picnic: What Endures

At the picnic, a fisherman
hauls waterweeds and an old
hat from the lake. A whisper
among the charcoal smoke:
"You shall not live forever."
Under bare feet, warmth of pine
needles as we climb
in bathing suits up a path
to the tower; icy damp
of its stairs. We never
touch, we'll never meet
again, but as we lean
together on the balcony, I
glimpse eternity beneath
her pale green suit:
small breasts, pink nipples.

Walking Home after the First Encounter

With scissors she snipped the blue
unbraidable cord, and we hanged
my salty shadow from a maple branch.

Beneath its dance of shudders
I saw the hole gulp the bone
and thank the barking dog.

We turned away, that frightened
beast and I, to walk beneath
arterial, throbbing stars.

And where the cow's tongue
ticked the hours, we watched,
from a black thicket, angels
lug to field's edge rocks of flesh.

The Migrant Camps

Sat in the car beside my doctor father
as the farmer's flashlight
guided us down a rutted
orchard road to a cluster of shacks:
smell of wine and kerosene, blare
of radio music. Watched as he
sewed up wounds from blade or bottle neck.

A sunny morning in August:
we walked past men on high ladders,
buckets at their waists,
women and kids stripping bright
fruit from the low branches;
stood and witnessed, then
signed the certificate
for a charred fingerbone protruding
from a heap of ashes and scorched tin.

Memorial Day

1

After our march from the Hudson to the top
of Cemetery Hill, we Boy Scouts proudly endured
the sermons and hot sun while Girl Scouts
lolled among graves in the maple shade.
When members of the veterans' honor guard
aimed their bone-white rifles skyward and fired,
I glimpsed beneath one metal helmet
the salmon-pink flesh of Mr. Webber's nose,
restored after shrapnel tore it.

2

Friends who sat near me in school died in Asia,
now lie here under new stones that small flags flap
beside.
　　　It's fifth-grade recess: war stories.
Mr. Webber stands before us and plucks
his glass eye from its socket, holds it high
between finger and thumb. The girls giggle
and scream; the awed boys gape. The fancy pocket watch
he looted from a shop in Germany
ticks on its chain.

After a Death

I heard the front door close
and from my window saw
my father cross the moonlit lawn
and start up the orchard road.
Then I was with him,
my mittened hand in his,
and Peter, my brother, his dead son,
holding his other hand.
The way the three of us walked
was a kind of steady weeping.

Driving Home after a Funeral

The boy watched the sun
set: gold seed squeezed
in the mountain's cleft beak
until it bled. He sat,
distant in the back-
seat, unable to move.
When the moon rose
its blue light formed
patches of mold
on his father's shoulder.
In the dark, a wadded
Kleenex his mother pressed
against her cheek
was a white snail
eating holes in a leaf.

Song of the Invisible
Corpse in the Field

And still I lie here,
bruised by rain, gored
by the tiny horns
of sprouting grass.

I hum the song of spiders
drawing, across the blankness
of my eyes, accurate maps
for the spirit's quest:
always death at the center
like Rome or some oasis
toward which all paths tend.

I am the absence
under your feet, the pit
that opens, toothed with dew.

Spring Floods

1

Later that week, when the reddish
silt-laden water subsided,
we found a deer
high in a tree, wedged
there by the flood: its legs
outstretched as if leaping,
its neck snapped and fallen
back along its flank.
It was my dead brother:
his body lifted, held
forever in the arms
of my twelfth year.

2

In a muddy field:
an open coffin
only I could see;
it was a boat my mother
sent to fetch me,
just as she sent the flood.
Water roiled so deeply
who could calm it
as she once did,
laying her cool hand
on my forehead in the dark
room before sleep?

In Haiti

1. SUNSET AT DESCHAPELLES

From the houses of American engineers
laughter and the sound of ice
in glasses. The pastor sets out benches
on the tennis court; it's time to sing
hymns in Creole: "Rock of Ages"
in this land where soft stone crumbles.

Mennonite nurses move through the twilight
toward their bungalows. Sweet reek
of jasmine; stench of mango rinds
and urine in the cactus hedge.
Red ants gather on a lizard's eye.

2. AT THE SPRING

I am the boy perched in the high
branches of a flamboyant tree,
hidden by its scarlet blossoms
and frondlike leaves. I watch
a Haitian girl squat to fill
her calabash at the gurgling spring
in the gully. She corks the bright
green gourd, hoists it to the cloth
pad on her head. Poised as a queen
under a heavy crown, she passes
beneath me with long, flat strides
and climbs a path that centuries
of naked feet have rubbed
thigh-deep in a limestone cliff.

3. BOY ON THE REEF/INFINITY OF DESIRE

Three feet below his belly, the reef's
lipped ridge, its last ledge
of coral; then sand sloping steeply
off into dark.
             Blue of his speargun
before his eyes, gulp of air
through the snorkel, and as he dives
the face mask pressing tight...
                          Down
through a shimmering curtain
of minnows, past the fish
he seeks, past ragged purple
sea fans, past conchs pink as cunts.

4. THE PALACE OF SANS SOUCI

A mapou's massive trunk
presses against a palace
wall; in a hundred years
both will fall.
             In his Citadel
on the mountaintop, mad
King Christophe sleeps,
a gold bullet in his skull.

Through which ruined arch
did my family pass?
In a sun-filled courtyard
I call and call.

I pass the old beggar who sits,
sucking on a corncob pipe, in the shade
of a huge gray mapou tree,
its roots stuck with candle stubs,
gifts for the ghosts inside;

down the hill past the stench
of the courtyard where burros are tethered,
across the parched lawn where kin
of the sick squat beside charcoal
fires cooking rice and red beans;

up the steps and through a double set
of screen doors that never yet kept
malaria out. Mother, I'm coming,
down the halls toward the room
where you lie, coughing and soon to die.

And if I had known, as no one
did, that this would be the last visit, what
could I have brought? All I have:
the sweat and sights and smells
of Haiti under my small straw hat.

Song: Early Death of the Mother

The last tear turns
to glass on her cheek.
It isn't ice because,
squeezed in the boy's hot
fist, it doesn't thaw.
It's a tooth with nothing
to gnaw; then a magical
thorn: prick yourself
with it, thrust it in soil:
an entire briery
kingdom is born.

The Weeds

On the lawn, beside the red house
she taught me to slice deep
circles around dandelions
with the sharp point of my trowel
so when I pulled them
the taproots came up too.

She wore a blue dungaree jacket,
her braided hair
tied in a paisley bandanna.
We crouched there near each other,
mother and son, digging in silence
in the dusk of late summer.

A Half-Dead Black
Cherry Tree across
the Road from
My Childhood House

Remnant of some lost orchard,
we climbed you for the few
bunches of fruit you produced;
beneath our feet branches snapped
exposing the soft white rot.
You became a part
of the fenceline: amber resin
oozed from your bark
where wire was stapled.
You closed on each strand
like a horse's mouth
on a bit: puckered scar
where you took it in
toward your slow heart.

Three Songs

I was in the fields.
God was a rock in my hands.

From such heaviness
what could rise?

Not his body,
only its cry.

2. ABRAHAM'S SONG

> *And he took the fire in his hand and a knife,*
> *and they went, both of them together.*
> GENESIS 22:6

Here there is no light
for the dark to lean on,
as an old man on his only son.

When the wings of the lungs
lift, air enters.

I can't call it hope,
though no blood was shed.

I can't call it grief,
yet the wound won't close.

Much sobbing, but no tears.
Lift up your eyes, God said,
this knife shall guide you.

3. SONG OF THOMAS, CALLED "THE DOUBTER"

Show me, I said, what
my fingers touch is true.

Then a wound appeared in air itself,
like a tear in blue fabric,

and I put my hand through,
into the other world.

There

When Trakl crossed over, the angels
accused him of the same poem
again and again. He held up
the face God gave him
and showed them the deep and lovely
line a single, recurring tear,
sliding earthward,
carved on a stone cheek.

Beggar's Song

Here's a seed. Food
for a week. Cow skull
in the pasture; back room
where the brain was:
spacious hut for me.

Small then, and smaller.
My desire's to stay alive
and be no larger
than a sliver
lodged in my own heart.

And if the heart's a rock
I'll whack it with this tin
cup and eat the sparks,
always screaming, always
screaming for more.

Swamp Songs

for Trisha

1

I'm glad when my boots sink
deep in the ooze
and to pull loose, against the smooth
suck, I grab
thick tufts of swamp grass.

2

On a wide hummock I kneel,
bend close, and watch my numb
forearms and hands: pale
herbivorous dinosaurs
that yank and chew
huge mouthfuls of cress
at the languid delta.

3

We lie at dusk on the naked
bank, watching as a red-winged
blackbird perches on a cattail stalk
and a muskrat paddles slowly
through weedy shallows toward its mound.

Indian Summer

At dawn, from the bedroom window: the elm tree's
shadow white with frost. Brief, strange sight; when I returned
with coffee for my wife, the lawn was green again.

—

The juniper along the fenceline blue with fruit.
The pear tree nude, its brown and gold windfall
rotting around it. The woodpile built.

—

Sparrows and juncos squabble in the holly bush.
Though the ground is cold, my body longs
to lie in yellow poplar leaves, warmed by the sun.

After the Guest

for my brother

The guest departs;
it was the briefest
of visits. While my wife
sleeps, I stand at the sink
washing dinner plates
that are smooth as the masks
my grief once wore.
Hot water on my tense hands,
soothing as tears.
On the wall there's a photo
of the dead one that I've fed
with my looking
as my wife feeds guests.
When she stirs in her nap,
when she moans or sighs,
it's no hungry ghost the night
has sent, but the simple cold.
I tuck a blanket
around her shoulders;
I pray we'll grow old.

Reading Late in the Cottage

There aren't that many pages left.
I'm getting nervous: What if
the author means to surprise me
by leaving the last twenty blank?
Now all sounds disturb me:
embers letting fall on the hearth
their heavy gray petals;
cattle outside, tearing the grass
with their teeth; and close by,
the screech of the luminous
insect trapped in the lightbulb.

The Caged Owl

1

Cage wires white like ribs
in my flashlight's glare.
Inside the heart lives on,
dark and feathered.

Swallowing small things
whole, it spits up
what it can't digest:
pellets of fur and bone.

2

Today I reread the history
of my childhood:
how a hand was cut off
and an owl claw attached.
"Mouse, mouse," I cried.
Love is what I sought.
"Hunger," they called it.

Friday Lunchbreak

At noon, still wearing their white
plastic helmets and long smocks,
they leave the frozen slabs
of calf hanging from aluminum
hooks on the loading docks
and stride down the street
past my window, headed
for the bank on the corner.
I remember the gray calf we found
last spring in Virginia, hidden
by its mother in a gully;
at six days it scampered
and wobbled.
           We watched
it grow heavy and slow, until
half a year later, fouled
with its own shit and dull of eye,
it stood with the other cattle,
hock-deep in muck by the barn.

Then it was gone, perhaps north
to this gallows place, where the men
tromp back, grinning, some with bottles
in brown paper sacks, these men
in spattered white smocks
who are as thick and wide
as the sides of beef they hug
and wrestle, angels of meat.

Virginia Backyard: July

Waking late, still inside a humid
heat-drenched dream that's not unlike
Keats's "sweet unrest," I walk
out past the fence where purple morning
glories have closed up into tight
buttons of color. Wild strawberry
plants I picked this spring are mostly
covered now by a thick new growth
of honeysuckle; kept from sun
the patch won't last. An indigo
bunting pauses on a dogwood twig.
Folding back golden petals, a sunflower
permits a first honeybee to wade
the wide, uneven expanse of a seedface
that spirals to a lime-green, pubic tuft.

On the Lawn at Ira's

for Ira Sadoff

Six years ago in Ohio we argued free will
versus fate as we weeded your garden
and hosed out a mole tunneling toward corn.
Your father walked out when you were thirteen
and everything you'd since done you called
an act and measure of your will.
At twelve, I killed a brother by accident,
my mother died soon after: my whole life
I sensed as a lugged burden
of the invisible and unforgiving dead.

Now we're sitting on a summer lawn in Maine.
The sun's out; it's the same argument
but I see it another way: you never
let the early hurt be felt and so
it governs you; I now admit I'm mostly
happy, even feel blessed among so many friends.
Hearing a sharp "thump" we investigate
and find a least flycatcher
stunned in the grass below a window.
I hold it in my palm: its small hot heart
beats so rapidly its whole body heaves.
We sit down and continue talking; the bird
lies there with one wing awry, shits in my hand,
stares up with a glazed eye. Ten minutes later
it pulls in its wing, tries to grip
with its tiny feet my too-large finger.
While we talk, joke, and argue
it suddenly flies, unwavering, away.

A Story Sassetta Paints

for my father

In the background a saint walks a path
through mountains and a centaur-haunted
forest. In the foreground he's arrived.
He greets a hermit at a cave's mouth.
They've dropped their cudgels
in the stony road, and as they hug
their two halos are one.

That's all. Let's say they're men,
not saints: what's taking place
is a wished-for, believable miracle
whose wishing must suffice.
When the one enters the gloomy cave
he cannot emerge, nor can
the other, making his way
through the world's woods, ever arrive.

Leaving the Asylum

The metal harps of the high gates
make a clangorous music
closing behind me. They
announce the "new life" of freedom
and only a battered valise
to lug down this alley of poplars.
I repeat the litany of the poem
that released me.
                Hollow tree
though I am, these things I cherish:
the hum of my blood, busily safe
in its hive of being; the delicate
oily kiss my fingertips give
each thing they touch; and desire,
a huge fish I drag with me
through the wilderness:
I love its glint among the dust and stones.

An Abandoned, Overgrown Cemetery in the Pasture near Our House

March; Virginia

All last winter, starved cattle
trampled a muddy flatness
around it, stretched their throats
over the low stone wall,
its top set with chunks
of quartz like teeth in a jaw.
Inside, vines cover the five
small cherry trees; brambles
everywhere. And the abyss
with its lips of weather
has already kissed away
the names carved on the stones.

—

I clear it with clippers,
slicing the prickly stalks
and tossing wiry tangles
of briars over the wall
to the cows.
            It's a warm day.
Working, I sluff off winter's
torpor as a snake sheds skin.
I find a wren's nest, cup
from which ghosts sip.

What's in it? Human tears,
their only food. Always it's empty,
always it's filled to the brim.

from

We Must Make a Kingdom of It

1986

and

New & Selected Poems

1988

We Must Make a Kingdom of It

So that a colony will breed here,
love rubs together two words:
"I" and "she." How the long bone
of the personal pronoun
warms its cold length against her fur.

—

She plants the word "desire"
that makes the very air
amorous, that causes the light,
from its tall stalk, to bend down
until it almost kisses the ground.

—

It was green, I saw it — tendril
flickering from dry soil
like a grass snake's tongue;
call it "flame" — light
become life, what the word
wants, what the earth
in its turning
yearns for: to writhe and rise up,
even to fly briefly
like the shovelful over
the gravedigger's shoulder.

Poem in New York

The derelict who lives on our street
looks like Whitman as a young man.
This summer he slept discreetly
in a greasy bundle of rags by the alley
trash cans. Now autumn's here, and at night
he sprawls in the warm, sugary gust
vented from the candy store.

—

I sat on the wharf's splintered pilings
and watched the corpse
pulled from the water. Its face glowed
the blue of lapis lazuli.
Two policemen wrapped the swollen
thing in plastic sheeting,
heaved it into the truck
and slammed the green door shut.

—

I listened with the other young poets
that day in the classroom
as Auden, wrinkle-skinned, unresponsive,
recited word for word an essay he wrote
thirty years before: "Your task
is like a mining engineer's —
how to get buried ore out of the ground.
And you can't use magic."

How many times
I've met my double on a New York street —
always he smiled and held out his blue hand
in greeting.

Who, if not he, bends to lift
the rotting body out of the Hudson? Who steps lightly
over the sleeper at rest in his redolent cloud?

Visit to the Island of Lost Souls

with apologies to H.G. Wells

1

I was a leopard caught by a demented
scientist. With drugs and electricity
he evolved me a million years
in a single week. You could say I raced
to the top of a Darwinian pyramid
that ends in man (above, only
the stars and the dark). I mean:
I look a lot like you, though
my eyes are odd, and I think
exactly like you — though my brain
isn't always quick enough
to stop my catlike reflex
and that may be my downfall,
as when I've chosen the wrong fork
at dinner and rather than blush
and mutter like the others around me
I plunge my butter knife
into the nearest human heart,
or my own if no one's near.

2

This is the ex-leopard talking again:
Did I tell you I write poetry?
Not that crap that rhymes in a hapless
effort to civilize with jingles,
and not the savage stuff full of growls
you probably expect, given my background.
I'm trying to express what it's like

to press up against the terror
of self-consciousness, to feel
its icy fur against my new, clean-shaven face.

A Shelf Is a Ledge

I don't understand by what perversity
Darwin and Saint Paul are kissing cousins
on my shelf. And how they both lean against
an encyclopedia of history...
It must give them bad dreams.
I watch Saul topple from his horse, but
Paul's all right. Darwin in the underbrush
glimpses a finch. And then there's that damned
history book ticking all night
like a cheap clock while it adds
the day's events to its late blank pages
and erases the early ones so it has
more space...
                    It's true a sane man
would resist the temptation to animate
dead things of the object world, and
such a shunning proves he's sane. Myself,
I hear a blessed humming in my head
and I'm its glad amanuensis.
Paul's taught me this: Love passes
understanding. And Darwin's on my side
as he screams in the dark: Survive! Survive!

Poem

The truth's in myth not fact,
a story fragment or an act
that lasts and stands for all:
how bees made honey in a skull.

Nantucket Morning/This World

All night I dreamed of heaven:
a blue space I drifted through, huge
enough to store everything.
                              Far below
I saw *this* world—pearl
of great price; "Body," Love said,
"is the only boat
from which you can dive to find it."

                    —

Naked, you wade toward shore
through low waves and sunlit foam.
I'm there to wrap a towel about you,
then my arms.
                    Beyond the dunes
whose curve and swell a landward longing
of the wind has shaped, there are leeward
clefts where pink, fragrant clumps
of the old rose, Aphrodite's
flower, take root.
                    And below,
scrub-pine woods are already
resinous with morning heat. On a bed
of needles, an upturned scallop
shell, its fluted rim lipped with dew.

Chateaubriand on the Niagara Frontier, 1791

He could be just one more erstwhile aristocrat lightfooting it
from the guillotine who's crossed the Atlantic to research
Rousseau's wonders of nature at first hand. And he is, but
tonight, writing in his travel journal, he'll make his own contri-
bution: the invention of the literary beauty of moonlight. It's a
concept destined to fascinate and console the melancholic
children and love-starved wives of the bourgeoisie he loathes.

It happens because he can't stand the smell of the frontier
inn where he's stopped for the night: an earth-floored room
with a fire in the middle. Everyone lies crowded together with
their feet near the embers, their bodies radiating out, Indian
and trapper alike. In a dream he can't share, they become greasy
spokes of a great, breathing wheel. The wheel lifts itself upright,
moves, then begins to roll along a rutted trail, deeper and deeper
into the new world.

Elegy

for James Wright

Not only doesn't the Ohio
stop tonight, it moves more
easily under the stars,
under the barge lights.
And in my veins
blood, though heavy
with sorrow, still flows.
And below the Catskills
the Hudson keeps flowing—
my own river, that's deeper
than anyone dreams
with its rich secret
of fish intact under
all that sewage and grief.

On the Hudson's far shore
there's a chestnut—
my own tree—a plank
fort hid in its branches.
Your poems taught me it
was there, though it's nothing
like your own tree by your own
river's bank—that sycamore,
pure thing so like the simple
word you sought, tree
from which the gray bark
peels and drops until
it stands half
in rags, half in radiance.

Reverie

I'm not going anywhere;
I'm actually sitting
at my desk, but I see
the sun touching the mountain,
and I feel the bookcase
beside me, tall and dark
with tomes. Then there's
the window itself —
a widow in both worlds.

The Pond

Snapping turtles in the pond eat bass, sunfish,
and frogs. They do us no harm when we swim.
But early this spring two Canada geese
lingered, then built a nest. What I'd
heard of, our neighbor feared: goslings,
as they paddle about, grabbed from below
by a snapper, pulled down to drown.
                                    So he stuck
hunks of fat on huge, wire-leadered hooks
attached to plastic milk-bottle buoys.
The first week he caught three turtles
and still there are more: sometimes he finds
the bottles dragged ashore, the wire
wrapped several times around a pine trunk
and the steel hook wrenched straight as a pin.

November

Unable to sleep, I spend the predawn hours
browsing. Paul talks, in Corinthians, about
the Lamb of God: unless the dead are raised
there is no Christ, no heaven. In Plato's
Phaedrus, the soul, imprisoned in a body,
painfully grows wings, longs to mount skyward
toward the world of Forms.
                                 But desire's
my god and resides in *this* world,
floating at night on a sea of ghosts
that rises and falls, sorrowful water
pulled by the moon.
                            And at dawn, desire's
there in the white field below my window
where three cows kneeling make small
green spaces around them with their body heat,
shapes in the frost like hopeful boats.

The Demonstration

Democratic National Convention,
Atlantic City, New Jersey, 1964

They bob above us all afternoon—
three giant charcoal portraits
of Goodman, Schwerner, and Chaney,
civil rights martyrs whose tortured
bodies have just been found
in the red clay wall
of a dam in rural Mississippi.

Staring up at their flat, larger-
than-life faces, I envy the way
they gaze at the gray ocean
and the gray buildings
with the calm indifference
of those whose agonies are over.
Myself, I'm a frightened teenager
at my first demonstration,
carrying a placard that demands
the seating of a mixed delegation
from a Southern state.

         No one
prepared me for the crowd's hostility,
the names we're called.

Still, we chant the slogan reason
proposed: "One man, one vote."
And still it holds—the small shape
we make on the dilapidated boardwalk—
reminding me now of the magic circles
medieval conjurers drew
to protect themselves from demons
their spells had summoned up.

On a Highway East of Selma, Alabama

July 1965

As the sheriff remarked: I had no business being there. He was right, but for the wrong reasons. Among that odd crew of volunteers from the North, I was by far the most inept and least effective. I couldn't have inspired or assisted a woodchuck to vote.

In fact, when the sheriff's buddies nabbed me on the highway east of Selma, I'd just been released from ten days of jail in Mississippi. I was fed up and terrified; I was actually fleeing north and glad to go.

—

In Jackson, they'd been ready for the demonstration. After the peaceful arrests, after the news cameras recorded us being quietly ushered onto trucks, the doors were closed and we headed for the county fairgrounds.

Once we passed its gates, it was a different story: the truck doors opened on a crowd of state troopers waiting to greet us with their nightsticks out. Smiles beneath mirrored sunglasses and blue riot helmets; smiles above badges taped so numbers didn't show.

For the next twenty minutes, they clubbed us, and it kept up at intervals, more or less at random, all that afternoon and into the evening.

Next morning we woke to new guards who did not need to conceal their names or faces. A little later, the FBI arrived to ask if anyone had specific complaints about how they'd been treated and by whom.

But late that first night, as we sat bolt upright in rows on the concrete floor of the cattle barn waiting for mattresses to arrive, one last precise event: A guard stopped in front of the ten-year-old black kid next to me. He pulled a FREEDOM NOW pin from the kid's shirt, made him put it in his mouth, then ordered him to swallow.

That stakeout at dusk on Route 80 east of Selma was intended for someone else, some imaginary organizer rumored to be headed toward their dismal, godforsaken town. Why did they stop me?

The New York plates, perhaps, and that little bit of stupidity: the straw hat I wore, a souvenir of Mississippi.

Siren-wail from an unmarked car behind me — why should I think they were cops? I hesitated, then pulled to the shoulder. The two who jumped out waved pistols, but wore no uniforms or badges. By then, my doors were locked, my windows rolled. Absurd sound of a pistol barrel rapping the glass three inches from my face: "Get out, you son of a bitch, or we'll blow your head off."

When they found pamphlets on the backseat they were sure they'd got the right guy. The fat one started poking my stomach with his gun, saying, "Boy, we're gonna dump you in the swamp."

It was a long ride through the dark, a ride full of believable threats, before they arrived at that hamlet with its cinderblock jail.

He was very glad to see it, that adolescent I was twenty years ago. For eight days he cowered in his solitary cell, stinking of dirt and fear. He's cowering there still, waiting for me to come back and release him by turning his terror into art. But consciously or not, he made his choice and he's caught in history.

And if I reach back now, it's only to hug him and tell him to be brave, to remember that black kid who sat beside him in the Mississippi darkness. And to remember that silence shared by guards and prisoners alike as they watched in disbelief the darkness deepening around the small shape in his mouth, the taste of metal, the feel of the pin against his tongue.

It's too dark for it to matter what's printed on the pin; it's too dark for anything but the brute fact that someone wants him to choke to death on its hard shape.

And still he refuses to swallow.

Solitary Confinement

Hayneville, Alabama, 1965

Even as the last bars clang
shut and I start to rub the purple ache
clubs left on shoulders, ribs,
and shins, my mind is fashioning
an invisible ladder,
its rungs and lifts of escape.

They've taken the SNCC pamphlets
but let me keep a book
of Keats — poems reminiscent
of my sad, adolescent affair
with the coffin-maker's daughter,
which taught me many things,
including carpentry.

        And when, at dusk,
the trusty held for car theft brings
my tray of grits and fatback,
it won't matter so much that,
groaning and puking,
I'll be sick for hours.

Imagination is good wood; by midnight
I'll be high as that mockingbird
in the magnolia across the moonlit road.

Hotel St. Louis, New York City, Fall 1969

When I went inside, the manager said, "You don't want to live here, kid." And even naive as I was I could see, looking at the people in the lobby, it was a violent place. I told him I didn't have much money and he said, "This place is for junkies and hoods; go to the St. Louis—that's winos and they're harmless," and he wrote out an address and slipped it under the bulletproof plastic window that covered his small booth.

He was right: In the five months I lived there, no one ever harmed me. I got an 8-by-10 room with a bed, a sink, and a dresser for $15 a week. That left me twenty for food.

My room was on the second floor, with a window on the air shaft. Next door, in an identical room, lived a bedraggled redhead named Beatrice Tiffany and her boyfriend Joe, a security guard. Whenever I caught a glimpse of him staggering, bleary-eyed and unshaven, down the narrow hall in his gray uniform and thick black belt, I prayed he wasn't allowed to carry a gun on the job or, worse yet, to bring one home. Tiffany's grown son, Eddie, and his boyfriend, Albert, lived in that tiny room too, sleeping on a mat on the floor.

What separated us was so thin it was more like a veil than a plaster wall. Whatever happened in their world happened in mine.

Luckily, we were on different schedules: Working six nights a week in a bookstore, I missed most of their family dramas. Mornings, when I was in, my neighbors were either sleeping it off or gone. I'd wake around six, piss in the sink, then boil water for coffee on the stove at the end of the hall.

All morning, I worked on my writing: drafts of poems, dream narratives, stray ideas. Around noon, I'd make two peanut-butter sandwiches, then, in midafternoon, leave for work. In the evening at the bookstore, I'd have a ham-and-cheese sandwich, a piece of pound cake, and a carton of milk. I never varied that routine, telling myself the lettuce in my deli sandwich was the daily green I needed and that the milk made it a balanced diet. Still, I lost two teeth that fall; they simply crumbled and fell out.

One week I was working on an idea to strengthen my memory by going back to the house where I lived when I was ten. Sitting on my hotel bed, I'd close my eyes and be standing on the front walk. To my right was the mountain ash with its orange berries; behind me, to the left, my mother's gray-and-white Chevy parked under the huge weeping birch whose feathery branches brushed its roof. As I walked up the steps I saw the white lattice of the porch and the hole beneath it where the dogs had burrowed. I entered and walked from room to room, pausing every few feet to notice as many details as I could: the worn cane seat of a chair, the color and pattern of a hooked rug my mother had made, the cover of a particular book in the library.

I could only make this journey twenty minutes at a time before my head started to buzz and I had to stop. Each day that week, I repeated my walk, concentrating on a different room and remembering more details each time. There was only a single place—one whole wall of the living room—where I couldn't see anything and found myself wincing and turning away no matter how many times I tried to look.

Late that week I woke up knowing I'd lost control of my mind. Thoughts whizzed by and my head felt light and impossibly intense. This had been my goal—to change my consciousness, but now that it had happened I was terrified. The last small voice of my sanity said: "Don't panic. Get food. Food will bring you down."

I fled the hotel to find a coffee shop. As I passed the supermarket on Broadway, a man in a butcher's white smock yelled, "Watch out!" and pushed by me with a silver shopping cart in which stood the entire carcass of a lamb, complete with blind eyes in a bloody head.

I ate and felt calmer; returned to the hotel, slept, and woke feeling normal. Next door, I heard Albert telling Beatrice how he'd walked ninety blocks to the Village to sell his blood, only to discover it was Saturday and the place was closed, so he turned around and walked back and now his feet hurt. Albert's voice sounded flayed and blank as the dead lamb's face, and I found myself saying out loud: "How can anyone so dumb survive?" But he did, of course; we all did somehow.

I slept again, and when I woke it was late that night and the whole hotel was partying. From all ten floors, confusion of loud musics and slurred shouts and, in the air shaft, the whistle and crash of empty wine jugs dropped from a hundred windows.

When I woke from my third sleep, it was morning and I heard the black janitor with his push broom in the alley, clearing a path through our jagged garden of glass. He worked quietly and quickly, and he wore, as he always did on Sunday mornings, a bright orange football helmet that glowed like the sun.

The Trick

I keep thinking of young Dostoyevsky, caught reading forbidden
books, talking about unlawful topics. First, he's put in prison,
then word comes that he's to be shot. He's hauled out into the
snow and roped to a stake, but it's a mock execution — at the last
moment a Cossack gallops up with a pardon from the Czar...

It's the sort of event that causes what is called a "break with
reality."

In a bar once I heard a story about a warden's bizarre hobby
and a prisoner who worked in the carpentry shop. The prisoner
lined a coffin with asbestos and pretended to die. That night, guards
came to his cell, hoisted the coffin with him inside, and carried
it out to the courtyard, where they attached it by wires to a col-
lapsed balloon. According to the usual instructions, they set the
coffin afire so hot air from the blaze began to fill the huge shape.

From his high window the warden watched as the whole
contraption lifted slowly into the night air and drifted over the
dark roofs to settle somewhere miles away beyond the walls.

The balloon is the soul; the blazing coffin's the body. The
trick is not to die.

Available Now:
Archaic Torsos of Both Sexes

Though I'm modest as most,
I couldn't help noticing
certain parts of the statues
have been polished
to a high sheen
by passing hands
as the centuries passed.
If it's a form of worship
it's not much odder
or more perverse
than the saint's stone toe
kissed to a stub by fervent lips.

And even though Plato
suspected art almost as much
as he suspected the body's curves,
he did assert Desire
could lead to the True
and Beautiful.
                    Therefore
I choose to believe that mortals
pausing here to cup a marble
breast or buttock
were doing their best
to grasp the Ideal,
and their foolish gestures
made it shine more brightly.

Lucky

Certain poems enclose
their own ecstasy
as that single ashen
case holds
the lovers of Pompeii.
We know it's lucky
to touch them.

—

Others, because of their vowels,
have the power to arouse
the soul from its torpor
and cause it to rise: moans
and sighs that become
bright threads of the fabric
a goddess weaves
by firelight, something
(as the hymn to Aphrodite goes)
"more golden and lovely than life itself."

After Botticelli's *Birth of Venus*

Aphrodite, foam-born, blown
shoreward on her wide shell
with the breeze tickling her bottom
and a large crowd gathered
on the beach to greet and gawk.
The authorities there, too —
men with large batons, trained
in mob control.
                              Someone
selling hot dogs and souvenir
brochures of the obvious.
Meanwhile the goddess herself
has that blissed-out, postcoital
expression that indicates
she's not all there — were she a boxer
with a decent manager he'd recognize
that look; right now he'd be
tossing in the towel, reaching
for a bright silk robe to wrap his pal.

The Fifth Month

1

This morning holds intact the skeletal
radiance of a dandelion's globe:
bones of delight a light wind
blows apart:
           the winged seeds lift:
a song whose burden is the earth,
lost to us even as we walk upon it.

2

Desire conceived you: Power that binds
to recombine, that makes,
from dust and bright-furred beasts,
a risen god, an upright ape.

3

Love's shrine is strewn with skulls
but where else worship you
through whom we enter the kingdom
of flesh a second time?

The Voyages

It's late when I try to sleep, resting
one hand on your hip, the other on my chest
where the rise and fall of breath
is a faint light that brightens and fades.
Today the doctor placed his stethoscope
against your belly and an amplifier
filled the tiny room with a scene
from old war movies — the submarine,
the churning of a destroyer's engines
fathoms above rapt, terrified sailors.
Child's heart, whose thrumming the doctor
pronounced as perfect as such things
can be guessed across such gulfs.

Here, deep in the night, I calm my fears
by choosing a place among Homer's crew,
lolling on Hades' shore. Inland, Odysseus
brims a trench with blood, extorts predictions
from the thirsty dead. But common sailors
already know that launchings and wrecks
make the same sounds: scrape of keel on rock,
loud cries. As for the rest,
we need our ignorance to keep us brave.

The Hand:
"Brightness Falls from the Air"

for my daughter at three months

Maybe you thought it was a bird
or some other strange and harmless
creature fluttering in attendance
as you lay on your back in the crib.

But today I watched as you held
your hand inches above your face,
gazed a long, unknowing moment
then suddenly understood its splayed
star-shape was yourself.

                    You screamed.
I lifted you up and held you close
and all the while I felt you
falling toward our world.

Tableau Vivant

It's the scene where Hector, reluctant,
leaves for his last battle.
That Achilles' spear will pierce his body
is a promise not yet kept;
it's still whole
beneath his wife's caress
for all its imperfections,
for all its healed wounds
that are like lips held tightly shut.

He hugs his wife. He lifts
his helmet plumed with horsehair
that here seems a child's toy
though in battle it will make him
taller than he is.

The Teachers

Too late, and only because of what happened, we reread the poem and broke the code. And then it seemed obvious the student meant to kill herself.

Tomorrow, I take my three-year-old daughter to visit the zoo. For the first time, she'll see her favorite animals — real lions and tigers. I worry that she'll be afraid, that what she thought was wonderful in picture books won't seem that way up close.

And what will I tell her? These are their real bodies? The bars are there because our curiosities are fatal; they protect us from that part of ourselves that's drawn toward the dangerous life within.

More likely I won't tell her anything, or what I tell her she'll forget. And she has eyes and can see for herself; she has a mind of her own and will decide.

"This is the zoo," I'll say, "where the animals live, if live they can."

The Western Invention
of Lyrical Nature

And there's Petrarch, our first
mountain climber, stumbling up
the slopes of Mount Ventoux
with his shepherd guide
and a bottle of wine — one more
trapped man of the Renaissance
looking for some way out
that doesn't lead to God.

It's almost dusk when he reaches
the summit. He's never gazed
so far, never known there was so large
a vista. He's standing there
for all of us, frightened but brave.
Biting his lip, he tastes the sea.

A Field in New England

What angel rolled it?
Releasing whom?
                    Where
is the cave?
            Everything
has become invisible
except this granite boulder
that blocked the door
to the tomb.

A Song

The other world's not for me—
I let my dead stroll there;
pale road, pale throat—
each of its pebbles
a white, vanishing note.
I far prefer minnow
and mole; I need to know
what their mouths know: round
stone in a stream, heart
buried in a box; to fetch
what's down there, black
and cold as a lump of coal.
To go that deep: ash and tear,
but to come back up: bud and leaf.

The Tree

1

The word does not share
the world's flaw ("leaf"
is complete, unscarred
by insect or wind-tossed twig),
yet it is an essence
that implicates the world
as a wound implies a body.

2

Each day the web made new—pattern
of line and space;
                    no matter
how tight the weave, emptiness
at the center.
                No matter how vast
the space, each long-drawn filament,
held fast to leaf and twig, is love.

3

Autumnal language: fullness and falling
away from the tree of self,
death with a future like seeds
in fruit...

          In spring I kneel
to find it: that word in earth
extending downward one root,
upward one leaf...

Not eyes
discover it, nor even fingers
touching and probing mud, but
mouth and tongue — to taste
this world on lips
where, for that instant, the world lives.

from

City of Salt

1995

Origin of the Marble Forest

Childhood dotted with bodies.

Let them go, let them
be ghosts.

      No, I said,
make them stay, make them stone.

A Litany

I remember him falling beside me,
the dark stain already seeping across his parka hood.
I remember screaming and running the half mile to our house.
I remember hiding in my room.
I remember that it was hard to breathe
and that I kept the door shut in terror that someone would enter.
I remember pressing my knuckles into my eyes.
I remember looking out the window once
at where an ambulance had backed up
over the lawn to the front door.
I remember someone hung from a tree near the barn
the deer we'd killed just before I shot my brother.
I remember toward evening someone came with soup.
I slurped it down, unable to look up.
In the bowl, among the vegetable chunks,
pale shapes of the alphabet bobbed at random
or lay in the shallow spoon.

A Moment

The field where my brother died—
I've walked there since.
Weeds and grasses, some chicory
stalks; no trace of the scene
I still can see: a father
and his sons bent above
a deer they'd shot,
then screams and shouts.

Always I arrive too late
to take the rifle
from the boy I was,
too late to warn him
of what he can't imagine:
how quickly people vanish;
how one moment you're standing
shoulder to shoulder,
the next you're alone in a field.

Everything

for my mother

Is this all life is then—
only the shallow breaths
I watch you struggle for?
That gasp right now—
if it was water
it would be such a small glass.

And I could lift your head
from the hospital pillow
and help you sip it
to comfort your parched
throat
into the ease of sleep.

Your agony makes no
sense when air
is everywhere, filling
this room where you lie
dying, where we move
as if in a trance, as if
everything were under water.

Elegy

Here are consoling pieties
like a tightly packed
warehouse
of mortuary statues
through which you
must elbow a path.

Here are sparrows
on a porch
sorting sand from seed
with their beaks.

Here's the hour
that has forgotten
the minute
though the minnow
remembers the stream.

Here are the roots
in one world
and the blossom
in the other.

A Dark Night

How I long to pull the old man in;
he's thrashing out there in the water,
he's drunk and can't swim.

Then again, maybe it's a dog
and he'll claw and bite me
as I lean from the small boat
to haul him up.

             The splashing
so near and those sounds —
are they growls
or a human's choked sobs?
How dark it is; how far I am from shore.

Who'd Want to Be a Man?

With his heart
a black sack
in which a small
animal's trapped.

With his grief
like a knot
tied at birth,
balled up and hard.

With his rage
that smashes the ten
thousand things
without blinking.

With his mind
like a tree on a cliff—
its roots, fists
clutching stone.

With his longing
that's a dry well
and where is the rain?

The Vase

Boredom and terror, and the older
I get the more terror arrives
dressed as boredom, wearing
the same clothes I wear to work
each day.

       Returning home, I empty
my pockets into a large vase
in the hall: bits of lint, scraps
of paper, loose change, a piece of string.

The vase is taller than I am,
blazoned with white chrysanthemums
and green, exotic birds in flight.

A la Mystérieuse

Only in books I knew you
or in dreams where,
elusive, you were the bit
of dress that disappeared
in the city filled with light
which I knew and did not
know, its streets
constantly shifting.
                    Nothing
prepared me to meet you,
to round a corner
and find you
whom Heraclitus worshiped,
dipping his hand
in the river of your hair,
letting the current
take it
to the small of your back.

The Gray Fox

Someone I know is dying at seventeen.
When he visited last Thanksgiving
he wore with an adolescent's joy
the black leather jacket I lent him.

Around us spring happens: a crocus
among the gravestones, plum blossoms
that open in a single night.

Already ivy twines the fencewire
and last year's path through the field
vanishes in the thick green of new grass.

It would be good to be the gray fox
that trots to pond's edge, spots me,
and stops. All winter he's hunted here,
undisturbed, and now he watches me
watch him, ten yards away, unafraid.

The Cliff

Below me treetops and a crow
making its slow progress.
The green canopy's no sea
or net, but that absolute —
thin veil between
the living and the dead.

Confusion of thickets behind me;
before me, open space.

From time to time returning
to this granite ledge
where I measure my life
by refusals, here
where measuring starts,
less than a step from the edge.

Self-Portrait at Twenty

I stood inside myself
like a dead tree or a tower.
I pulled the rope
of braided hair
and high above me
a bell of leaves tolled.

Because my hand
stabbed its brother,
I said: Make it stone.

Because my tongue
spoke harshly, I said:
Make it dust.
         And yet
it was not death, but
her body in its green dress
I longed for. That's why
I stood for days in the field
until the grass turned black
and the rain came.

Muse of Midnight

In the street, stars collide,
parts of their bodies
breaking off
like chunks of salt.

Still, you hold her,
you're not letting go.
She's the bright-colored
bird with real feathers
and a toy heart, or
toy feathers and a real
heart.

When all this started
you were lying on a couch.
Now you rise
through the ceiling,
now you're roiled in a cloud,
now you're rain falling
toward its target: a room in flames.

Tristan and Iseult

Tristan and Iseult had nothing
on me — shown a bonfire
I'd hop aboard
as gladly as if
it were an ice floe
drifting north,
and as fat dripped
from my bones
I'd be wrapping up
in aurora borealis
just to keep warm.

Fire and ice —
at that intensity
the distinction's lost.

Love or hate — who
can say
when the need's that deep?

On dark nights I'd
reach up toward her face —
sometimes it was the moon,
sometimes a radiant
ax-blade
descending to kiss my wrists.

After Piero di Cosimo's
Venus, Mars, and Amor

Naked on the ground
they both recline
in opposite directions.
The god's asleep,
the goddess lies awake,
smiling,
propped on an elbow,
her tilted face
held in her open palm.

In the background
wolves skulk
to their lairs,
tails close-curled
like soldiers
quitting a field
with banners furled;
as if the thrust
of this scene
is not the adage
that lust disrupts
but something
about its aftermath:
how the world's made safe
for one more day:
Venus's hares hopping about
Mars's discarded armor.

Glukupikron

to Sappho

Word you created
which we translate
"bittersweet"
            thereby
reversing the terms
as if we thought pain
came first
and pleasure only later;
for you maybe joy
was initial,
to be followed
by harsh disappointment.

Yet in the word itself
the two fuse,
and in the condition
it refers to
they mingle,
indistinguishable,
not to be separated
by any force.

It was
your word for love.

Lament

I thought of you
as I drove past
the girl kneeling
on the verge
by her upside-down
bicycle.

       I know
she was only
fixing the chain
but for one moment
I saw her playing
a round harp
(and I thought of you
as I drove past).

There on the highway's
edge where gusts
from passing cars
whipped the grass
like wind off the sea
and she was kneeling,
her arms moving
among the metal spokes
plucking from them
a music lost
in the louder
impersonal sound
of traffic (and I thought
of you
as I drove past).

The girl kneeling
on the verge,
adjusting the loop
of metal links
that would propel her
into the future,
but also playing
(and I thought of you
as I drove past)
a round harp
on a desolate coast.

Investigation

This much is known:
the thread you never
let go of
guided you back.
And when you emerged,
years later, light
hurt your eyes.
Blood on your rusted
blade was dry.

But what happened
in the labyrinth?
In deepest dark
you grappled,
felt its breath
on your face,
stabbed
and fled.
       A monster?
Wouldn't *anything*
cry like that,
pierced to the heart?

My Father's Voice

Even as I rage, I see my daughter
wince and cringe
as I did, too, ages ago,
as if braced
against sudden wind,
blinking quickly, then her face
going blank as a mask
while in the heart a green bush
weathers the shaping blast.

The Gift

for my daughter

Scissors, glue, clumsy
fingers — crude tools
I've used to make
this cardboard bird
I've painted bright
unlikely colors
and hung by a string
above your crib.

—

In last night's dream
you were grown
and I was old
and in the backyard
digging a deep hole.
You stood above me
shining a light
where I shoveled down
through all my life.

—

In an ancient book,
Bede wrote
how a sparrow flew
from dark through
a lighted meadhall
into dark again.

—

Tiny wings of your lungs —
each beat a breath.

Father's Song

Yesterday, against admonishment,
my daughter balanced on the couch back,
fell and cut her mouth.

Because I saw it happen I knew
she was not hurt, and yet
a child's blood's so red
it stops a father's heart.

My daughter cried her tears;
I held some ice
against her lip.
That was the end of it.

Round and round; bow and kiss.
I try to teach her caution;
she tries to teach me risk.

The City of Salt

In the sun-drenched
city of salt
where the window boxes
are little coffins
full of red geraniums,
flower
that offers up
earth's smell of death
like water
from a deep well.

In that city of salt
where my mother walks
with a basket
over one arm —
she's off to market,
she's going to buy
all those things
she forgot to give us
when she was alive.

In that city of salt
the sun never sets,
the rooms of her apartment
fill up
with vegetables:
the purple globes
of eggplant, asparagus
like the blunt bolts
a crossbow fires,
and peppers convoluted
as the heart
and sweet to taste.

from

Orpheus & Eurydice

2001

> *How can I celebrate love,*
> *now that I know what it does?*

The Entrance to
the Underworld

A common enough mistake:
looking in the wrong place.
It's not a fissure
in the earth, or crack
in a cliff face
that leads sharply down.

You were looking in the wrong
world. It was inside
you—entrance
to that cavern
deeper than hell,
more dark and lonely.
Didn't you feel it open
at her first touch?

When I first saw...

When I first saw her
she was so beautiful
I wanted to be a mirror
and hold all of her.
My eyes couldn't do that,
much as I tried
to calm them, saying:
"Drink deep of her face."

If I had become a lake...
A mirror is all surface
but a lake has depths.
I would have drawn her in,
undine or water nymph,
alive inside me.

A snake…

death of Eurydice

A snake no bigger
than a bracelet
of braided gold
unfastened and cast aside
in the haste of love…

The bite itself—only
the pinprick
you might feel
stepping barefoot
on the open clasp.

His Lament

How is it she lies here,
her body still
so warm it makes me wince?

How is it she's nothing now?

They say there's a god
who can squeeze mud
in his fist,
breathe on it and it lives.

And me? All I do is kneel
beside her corpse,
numbly repeating her name
as if
some nacreous alchemy
of the voice
could pearl a piece of dust.

If...

If your gaze takes in
the world,
a person's a puny thing.

If a person is all
you see,
the rest falls away
and she becomes the world.

But there's another world
into which a person
can disappear.

Then what remains?
Only your word for her:
Eurydice.

When I was alive...

Eurydice

When I was alive—only glimpses,
moments of bliss but
always the body resisting,
refusing to let
the soul go.

        In that world,
I was a fish too eager
to enter the nets; here,
I'm a river.

        There, I was a bird
hopelessly searching for its nest;
here, I'm a wind that blows
where it wishes and needs no rest.

When I died, all Orpheus heard
was a small, ambiguous cry.
How could he know how free I felt
as I unwound the long bandage
of my skin and stepped out?

I was moving…

Orpheus

I was moving down the bank
toward the boat, lost
in the mob of newly dead,
when scowling Charon
stepped from the mist
to grab me by my shoulder:
"You'll go no farther
till you're dead."

I thought: What's music
to a brute like this,
and yet the chord I struck
hit him like a blow.
His face softened.
He sat down right there
in the stinking mud,
chin propped on fists, listening.

When Eurydice saw him

When Eurydice saw him
huddled in a thick cloak,
she should have known
he was alive,
the way he shivered
beneath its useless folds.

But what she saw
was the usual: a stranger
confused in a new world.
And when she touched him
on the shoulder,
it was nothing
personal, a kindness
he misunderstood.
To guide someone
through the halls of hell
is not the same as love.

The Ghosts Listen to Orpheus Sing

He stood before the throne
and we stared, astonished,
at his breath pluming
in the cold air.

And then he strummed
his lyre and sang
the things we knew
and had forgot—
the earth in all its seasons
but especially spring
whose kiss melts
the icicle's bone
so that the dead bush
blooms again.

He sang the splendid wings
sex lends.

He sang the years passing
like sparks
flung in the dark:
anvil, tongs, and hammer
toiling at pleasure's forge.

Last of all it was loss
he sang, how like a vine
it climbs the wall,
sends roots and tendrils
inward,
bringing to the heart
of the hardest stone
the deep bursting emptiness of song.

My body was never marred

Persephone

My body was never marred;
no dart of Eros
ever pierced my skin.
Where my heart was
a pomegranate is —
how could I be moved?

And yet, as he sang,
I watched pale faces
in our hall of ghosts
swaying like a meadow
and memory blossomed.
I saw again
my lost companions
wandering in sunlight
in the upper air.
I walked among them
green and careless,
not hearing the rhythm
of his chariot approaching,
not yet caught
in the sickle
of his arm's curve.

At the field's edge
I searched for lilies;
never saw the god
whom love had ravaged,
myself the flower
he'd come to gather.

When they said...

Eurydice

When they said I must leave hell
and I put on flesh again,
it felt like a soiled dress.

And as I followed him
up the steep path
I kept staring at his feet,
callused, bleeding. How
could I once have held
and kissed them?

                  My sandal
came undone. I paused
for breath because
air hurt my lungs.

A hundred delays offered
their help, their hope,
but still the opening
grew until at last I saw
his body silhouetted
against the entrance glare:
dark pupil
of an eye that stared.

In the cave mouth…

Orpheus

In the cave mouth I stopped,
stunned, to lean against
a broken limestone tooth.

The light was like a wall
and I was afraid.
I turned to her as I had before:

to save myself.

She was something between
the abyss and me,
something my eyes could cling to.

Once the two of us

Once the two of us
were a single stream
flowing over
and around itself
as if our bodies
had no bounds
but were only
a liquid braiding
of currents
and sensuous eddies.

Now I watch her
pale form flee alone
back down
the precipitous path.
She's a waterfall
plunging over the lip
of a cliff:

     white foam
shattering on the rocks below.

In the shadows...

In the shadows at the clearing's
edge, wounded deer stood
and wild boar gored with spears
but not brought down,
and other animals, smaller,
whimpering among the branches.

One of them stepped forward,
approached the spot where Orpheus
was seated alone on a boulder.

It was a fox who, having caught
his paw in a trap,
had chewed it off.

        Bowing,
he said: "Enough
of maiming and blame.
We want to be lifted up
in song, our lost limbs
restored.
        Orpheus,
she was you in another body.
Bright threads bound you together.
Rise now and strike your lyre.
Sing what connects us,
what no tooth can sever."

His Grief

With my words
I'll make rocks
weep and trees
toss down
their branches
in despair.

In its heart
each object
guards a tear
so round
and absolute
it mirrors all
the passing scene.
Those clear globes
are the souls
of things.
I want to shatter
them. I want
to make them sing.

Far below, plowed fields...

Far below, plowed fields vibrated
in the spring heat like black harps.

But all that was behind him now:
the lakes and swamps, the low places,
the lilacs with their heart-shaped
leaves shading the clustered huts.

He turned to the windy cliffs
and pathless slopes above the tree line
where each boulder gave forth
its single, inconsolable note.

Who knows? Maybe it would be simpler.
When she was alive, her body
confused him; he couldn't think
clearly when she was close. Scent
of her skin made him dizzy.

Now, where she had been: only
a gaping hole in air,
an emptiness he could fill with song.

The Wedge

When there were two of us
there was one world

and one moon. When you
died, I was alone

in another world
whose two moons

of grief and rage
wax and wane

in the starless sky.
By their light,

all I eat becomes
ashes on my tongue.

Now I can't stand
to be touched

or to see anyone
touching. When I find

lovers, I set
this wedge between them:

love is no use,
though lovers are used;

who seeks to soothe
will only bruise.

His Dream:
The Black Tree/Thirst

I saw her, out past the first
waves, swaying
on an undulant stalk.

At my feet, she'd left
her wisdom and bones —
unsortable pile on the shore.

Then I was under a tree,
its trunk twined
with a thick helix of vine,
a twinned upthrusting,
its intermingled foliage
more green than black.

Stepping from the dark,
she held cupped hands
to my lips.
        "Everything
is risk," she whispered.
"If you doubt, it becomes
sand trickling
through skeletal fingers.
Believe, and it's water
from what deep well."

Fields took on…

Fields took on their final
green; the sea was still
as the sky.

        No longer
did clouds drift
toward the horizon
like shadows without bodies,
or like wings
without that
which they were meant to lift.

And the rose, whose rich
petals are saturated
with vanishing…

ABOUT THE AUTHOR

Gregory Orr is the author of seven previous collections of poetry, the most recent of which is *Orpheus & Eurydice* (Copper Canyon Press, 2001). His fourth book of criticism, *Three Strange Angels: How Lyric Poetry Transforms Trauma*, was published by the University of Georgia Press in their Life of Poetry series, and his childhood memoir, *The Blessing*, appeared from Council Oak Books. The recipient of National Endowment for the Arts and Guggenheim Fellowships, he has also been a Rockefeller Fellow at the Institute for Culture, Violence, and Survival. He has taught at the University of Virginia since 1975, where he is Professor of English and poetry editor of the *Virginia Quarterly Review*. He is also a columnist and editor of the magazine *Sacred Bearings: A Journal for Survivors*. He lives with his wife, the painter Trisha Orr, and his daughters in Charlottesville.

INDEX OF TITLES

INDEX OF FIRST LINES

The Chinese character for poetry is made up of two parts: "word" and
"temple." It also serves as pressmark for Copper Canyon Press.

Founded in 1972, Copper Canyon Press remains dedicated to publishing poetry
exclusively, from Nobel laureates to new and emerging authors.
The Press thrives with the generous patronage of readers, writers, booksellers,
librarians, teachers, students, and funders—everyone who
shares the conviction that poetry invigorates the language
and sharpens our appreciation of the world.

For information and catalogs:

COPPER CANYON PRESS
Post Office Box 271
Port Townsend, Washington 98368
360/385-4925
poetry@coppercanyonpress.org
www.coppercanyonpress.org

The font Filosofia is Zuzana Licko's interpretation of the work of Giambattista Bodoni. Without the extreme contrast of thick and thin that is characteristic of many Bodoni revivals, Filosofia feels fresh and contemporary. Book design and composition by Valerie Brewster, Scribe Typography. Printed on archival quality Glatfelter Author's Text at McNaughton & Gunn, Inc.